Portville Free Library
Portville, N. Y.

W9-BWS-987

Books by Sid Fleischman

Mr. Mysterious's
Secrets of Magic

Mr. Mysterious's
Secrets of Magic

by Sid Fleischman

Illustrated by Eric von Schmidt

WITH DIAGRAMS BY MR. MYSTERIOUS

AN ATLANTIC MONTHLY PRESS BOOK

LITTLE, BROWN AND COMPANY

BOSTON   TORONTO

DISCARDED FROM THE PORTVILLE FREE LIBRARY

TEXT COPYRIGHT © 1975 BY ALBERT S. FLEISCHMAN

ILLUSTRATIONS COPYRIGHT © 1975 BY ERIC VON SCHMIDT

ALL RIGHTS RESERVED. NO PART OF THIS BOOK MAY BE REPRODUCED
IN ANY FORM OR BY ANY ELECTRONIC OR MECHANICAL MEANS IN-
CLUDING INFORMATION STORAGE AND RETRIEVAL SYSTEMS WITHOUT
PERMISSION IN WRITING FROM THE PUBLISHER, EXCEPT BY A REVIEWER
WHO MAY QUOTE BRIEF PASSAGES IN A REVIEW.

FIRST EDITION

т 04/75

Some of these tricks have appeared in
slightly different form in *Cricket*.

Library of Congress Cataloging in Publication Data

Fleischman, Albert Sidney.
  Mr. Mysterious's secrets of magic.

  "An Atlantic Monthly Press book."
  SUMMARY: Diagrammed instructions for performing
twenty magic tricks such as "The Vanishing Ghost," "The
Lie Detector," and "Frankenstein's Toothache."
  1. Conjuring—Juvenile literature. 2. Tricks—Juve-
nile literature. [1. Magic tricks] I. Von Schmidt,
Eric, ill. II. Title.
GV1548.F6   793.8   74–28222
ISBN 0–316–28584–6

ATLANTIC–LITTLE, BROWN BOOKS
ARE PUBLISHED BY
LITTLE, BROWN AND COMPANY
IN ASSOCIATION WITH
THE ATLANTIC MONTHLY PRESS

*Published simultaneously in Canada
by Little, Brown & Company (Canada) Limited*

PRINTED IN THE UNITED STATES OF AMERICA

9/5 nuraga 76

For Stuart McLeod
The Wizard of Waban

Secrets

Introduction
or
How to Vanish an Elephant

SNAP YOUR FINGERS. I'll wait.

Done?

I'll tell you why in a moment.

Have you ever wondered how magicians *become* magicians? After all, there are few schools for sorcery in the Yellow Pages.

From Merlin to Blackstone, all the great wizards of the past began as you are beginning: with a book of secrets open before them.

Magicians teach themselves magic. But then, you have already taught yourself a lot of things: catching a ball, jumping rope, whistling and maybe wiggling your ears.

You may start with a simple coin trick and some-day vanish an elephant.

Magicians come in all shapes and ages. There have been famous magicians with short, plump fingers. Many are left-handed. And there are wondrous wizards no older than seven or eight.

I was ten when I first became interested in hokery-pokery. After learning a few tricks from a book I discovered the biggest secret of all. Unless I rehearsed in private I fumbled the trick in public.

A school play would be a shambles if the actors didn't first rehearse their parts. And a magician is a kind of actor playing the role of a wizard.

A wizard makes mystic passes with his hands. He utters magic words. He appears to be in command of uncanny powers. It's all pretense, of course, but that's part of the fun. Most of all, a wizard creates an atmosphere of things mysterious and surprising.

Surprising. There is a kind of suspense in watching a magic trick unfold. What's going to happen? And then — behold! It happens.

That's why a magician never tells you exactly what he's going to do before he does it. It would be like telling the end of a joke first.

Would you believe that there are thousands of magic tricks and sleights of hand? No one has ever counted them all and every day new ones are being invented. Some of the bafflers in this book are centuries old; others are original in whole or in part.

Pick the ones that you especially like. There are tricks for every taste. A favorite saying among magicians is that it is better to master six tricks than to perform a hundred badly.

Did you snap your fingers a moment ago? No trick in this book is harder to learn and most are easier!

I hope one day you will be vanishing elephants. I'll tell you how to start. First, catch one elephant . . .

Sid Fleischman

Penny on the Nose

DID YOU KNOW that you can pluck a coin from a friend's nose?

"Look! My hands are empty," you say. And they really are. Then you add, *"I'll need a penny for this trick. Ah, there's one —"*

You approach your friend and give his nose a tweak. Behold! A real penny tumbles out.

Lift an arm and drop a penny into the sleeve of your jacket. The coin will stay there as long as you don't lower your arm below your waist.

Now you are ready to amaze everyone. Hold up both hands and show them front and back. Even spread your fingers to prove that you are hiding nothing.

As you say that you need a penny, lower your arms. With the back of your hand toward the audience, cup your fingers. The coin will silently shoot down into your hand.

Try it right now and you'll be surprised at how easy it is to catch.

Don't make a fist around the penny. Just let it lie within your slightly cupped fingers.

Raise this hand to someone's nose, twist gently, and let the penny fall. Catch it in your other hand or a glass, which makes a fine noise. And say, *"I find more pennies this way!"*

Trick Tip

Don't watch your hand as it catches the coin from your sleeve. People will look where you look, and that would spoil the trick.

The I-Don't-Believe-It Trick

"This trick is so amazing," you say, *"that I don't believe it myself."*

As a matter of fact, it *will* amaze you when you try it. You cause a wooden matchstick to pass through the solid bar of a common safety pin. Visibly. Right before your eyes!

It's wonderfully easy to do. But first you'll have to set up the stick and pin as shown in the drawings.

First cut off the head of a kitchen match. You only need the stick.

Then carefully push the point of the pin through the center of the stick. The wood won't be as apt to

4

split if you soak the match in water for a minute or so.

Now close the pin and you are ready to fool yourself. Later you can fool your friends.

Hold one end of the pin firmly, as shown in the first drawing. Notice that the *left* half of the stick rests *below* the bar of the pin. That's important.

Clip the other end of the stick under your right thumb or fingernail. Snap downward and watch! The left half of the stick appears to jump through the iron bar.

Amazing? Try it before reading the secret below. Have the fun of fooling yourself first!

THE SECRET

Of course, the matchstick doesn't *really* go through the pin. That would be impossible.

Here's what really happens. When you snap one end of the match it spins around — too fast for the eye to see — and comes to rest *above* the bar of the pin.

In other words, you have caused the ends of the stick to instantly reverse positions. And that's what creates this startling I-don't-believe-it illusion.

If your fingernails are too short, you can strike the

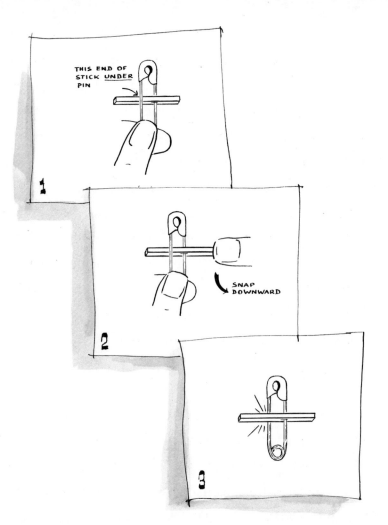

stick instead. Make sure it swings easily on the pin.

It may take you a minute to discover just how hard to snap the match. If you snap it too hard it may break, too lightly and it won't pivot all the way around. You'll quickly get the feel of it.

Trick Tip

Magicians almost never repeat a trick. With the element of surprise gone, your friends may catch on. But this trick is so foolproof that you can repeat it. In fact, it becomes even more baffling when you do it again.

So try this. Clip your fingernail under the end of the match and snap upward. Behold! The amazing stick passes back through the pin.

The Vanishing Ghost (Almost)

YOU HOLD a white, ghostly creature in your fist. With a toss of your arm the ghost vanishes — almost. Everyone can see a telltale bit of the ghost still hanging from the bottom of your fist.

"Oh, that," you say, opening your hand. *"That's just the ghost's tailfeather."* The ghost has vanished.

You'll never guess where!

You make the ghost out of tissue paper or a paper napkin.

The ghost is in two parts. Carefully form a knot in one end — that's the head. Tear off the paper about an inch below the knot.

The ghost's tailfeather is a torn corner of paper an inch or so long.

When the two pieces are gripped in the fist, with the knot at the top, you appear to be holding a whole ghostly thing.

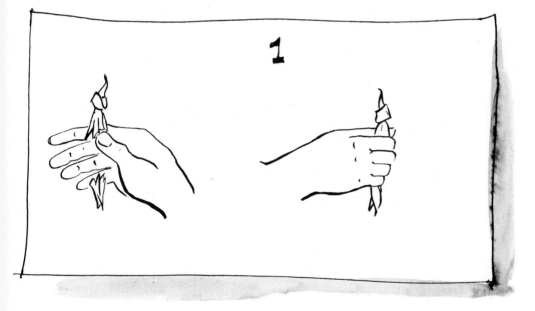

One more bit of preparation. You need a piece of sticky transparent tape. Form a small loop, *sticky side out.*

Flatten the loop and stick it behind the head of the ghost. That leaves an outside sticky surface — and that's what makes this trick work.

"This is my friend, *Archibald the Ghost,*" you say. Hold the creature so the tape is away from the audience and won't be noticed.

"*Archibald doesn't walk through walls. He jumps through ceilings. I'll show you.*"

If you are holding Archibald in your <u>right</u> hand,

10

turn your left side toward the audience. Toss your arm toward the ceiling and say, *"Jump, Archibald!"* Look upward.

Swing your arm again and repeat the command. Look upward. This sets a pattern of movement that catches your audience off guard for what you now do.

As you are about to start the third upward swing of your hand, *stick the head of the ghost to the right side of your trouser leg.* Don't hesitate or break the rhythm. Make the upward toss as before.

"Jump!" Then, *"Gone!"*

Pretend that you don't know that a bit of paper is still hanging from your fist.

"Right through the ceiling. Did you see that?"

The razzing starts. "It's in your fist! Open your hand!"

Finally, take notice of the exposed bit of ghost. *"In real life Archibald used to be a goose. That's just one of his tailfeathers."*

Tug out the bit of paper and open your fist. The ghost is gone.

Trick Tip

The knot of paper is stuck to the blind side of your trousers. You can't turn without exposing it. Here's what to do:

With the "tailfeather" on the palm of your left hand, blow it into the air. At the same time, drop your right arm in a relaxed, natural manner.

Get the knot in your hand while everyone is watching the bit of paper float to the floor.

Put your hand in a pocket, leaving the knot behind, and draw out a prop for another trick. A deck of cards, a rubber band, a piece of string — anything.

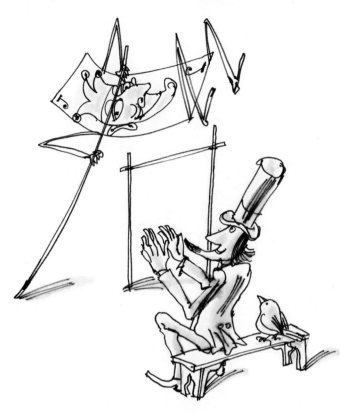

The Jumping Joker

YOU SHOW the joker and place it in the center of the deck.

"This is kind of a backwards trick," you say. *"You have to applaud BEFORE I do it. So if you will clap your hands, maybe the joker will take a bow. Ready? Applause, please."*

A card jumps off the deck and somersaults, landing face up. It is the joker.

Two secrets make this trick work. First, you do not actually place the joker in the center of the deck; you only make it look that way.

Show the joker and any other card behind it as if they were a single card. The drawing shows you how to hold the cards, bent slightly, so that they'll cling together perfectly.

"The joker," you say, and place the card(s) on top of the deck.

Then deal off the top card and slip it into the center of the pack. The joker is still on top! That's the first secret.

Now for the second. As you square the deck, pull back the top card less than a quarter of an inch.

Lay the deck on a table with the overlapping top card, the joker, toward you.

"Applause, please."

You clap too, but in a special way. If you rest the edges of your hands on the table, a few inches behind the deck, and slap your hands together *sharply* — watch! The gust of wind lifts the overlapping joker and causes it to somersault.

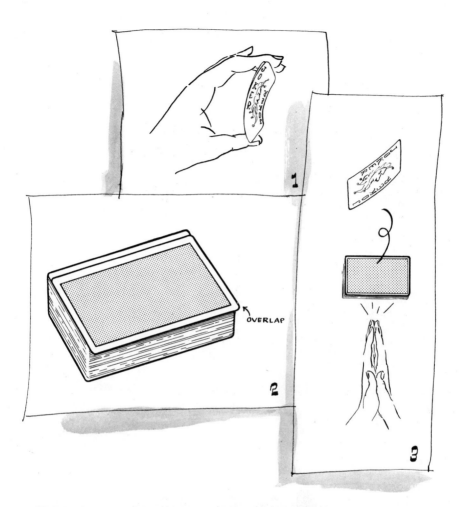

OVERLAP

How to Keep a Secret

It's hard to keep a secret. But there is one person you can tell — your best friend. Together you'll find it easier to keep magic secrets secret.

Frankenstein's Toothache

IN THIS BAFFLER, a ring is slipped onto one of your fingers. Then the ends of your fingers are tightly bound with a rubber band. The ring escapes in a way that *looks* impossible.

What has Frankenstein to do with it? You'll see.

16

You'll need a rubber band, a piece of string about a yard long, and a ring large enough to slip easily on and off your finger. A brass curtain ring will do, a plastic ring, a metal washer, or anything similar that you can find in the dime store.

"Did you know that Frankenstein's monster had a toothache?" you say, holding up the ring. *"The tooth looked like this. You can see that it had a big cavity."*

You thread the string through the hole and knot the ends. *"Dr. Frankenstein decided to pull the tooth with a piece of string. It was a back tooth, so I'll put it back here."*

You slip the ring onto the base of your middle finger. Hold your hand palm up and let the string hang below.

"The trouble was that the tooth began to ache something awful and the monster's jaws clamped shut. I'll show you with this rubber band."

Starting with your index finger, twist the rubber band from finger to finger. And that's when the secret comes in. You *skip* the finger with the ring.

Get a small rubber band now and try the secret twist.

You'll be surprised at the optical illusion. You can even stretch your fingers for a moment and all of them appear to be bound.

Of course, you don't let anyone see the back of your hand. It looks like the second drawing. You do the whole trick palm up.

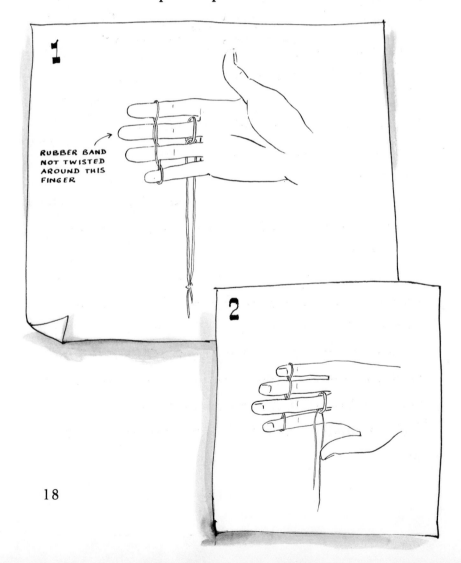

RUBBER BAND NOT TWISTED AROUND THIS FINGER

"With the monster's jaws locked shut, Dr. Frankenstein couldn't pull out the tooth."

Hand an end of the string to a friend.

"But he knew magic words. He said HOKERY-POKERY-ALAKAZAM and yanked. Out came the tooth!"

Quickly draw back your hand. The ring easily slips off your finger and will dangle free on the string.

Show the rubber band still entwined on your fingers. *"The monster never opened his mouth."*

For some reason, people don't suspect the rubber band. They think the trick is in the ring. While they are examining it, lower your hand, pull back your loose finger and slip it on top of the rubber band.

Now you can show the other side of your hand — the top. *"Of course, there's a hole in the ring. Don't you see it? The one in the middle."*

And you casually pull off the rubber band.

The Rattle, Rattle Coin

AMAZING! This trick not only fools the eye. It fools the ear.

Have a friend drop a coin into an empty match-box. After wrapping rubber bands around the box you begin to shake it. Everyone can hear the coin rattling inside.

"Catch!"

You toss the box. When your friend takes off the rubber bands and looks into the box — the coin has vanished!

Would you believe that the coin in the box doesn't do all the rattling? The sound comes from your sleeve, where you have another box and coin hidden.

Place a coin in this secret matchbox and fix it to the underside of your wrist with a rubber band. Let's say that it is your right wrist. The box is well hidden by your shirt or coat sleeve.

With two rubber bands in a left pocket you are ready to amaze your friends. Follow these easy steps:

1. After a friend drops the coin into a matchbox and shuts it, take the box in your right hand. Your left hand gets a rubber band out of your pocket.

2. Transfer the box to the left fingers and take the rubber band in the right. Wrap it around the narrow width of the box. In doing so, turn the box over so that the open side of the closed drawer faces downward. That's important, for you are about to steal the coin — crafty wizard! — under everyone's nose.

3. The diagram shows you how to hold the box at the edges. Give them a squeeze while wrapping the rubber band. Look what happens! The top and bottom buckle, and if you are holding the box

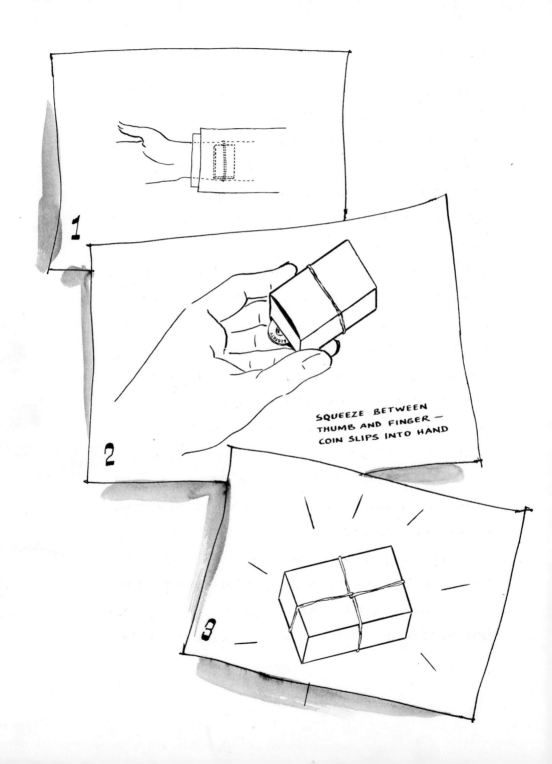

1

2

SQUEEZE BETWEEN
THUMB AND FINGER —
COIN SLIPS INTO HAND

3

slightly tilted — the coin slides out right into your waiting fingers.

4. Your left hand (now holding the coin) immediately goes to the pocket for a second rubber band. *At the same time* your other hand begins to shake the box. The coin rattles (from your sleeve), catching everyone's attention. Who would think you are stealing away the coin? It's still in the box — we can hear it!

5. Leave the coin behind in your pocket and remove the second rubber band. Wrap it lengthwise around the box.

6. That's all the hanky-panky you have to do. The right hand keeps shaking and rattling the coin. Say *"Catch!"* and toss the box to someone.

It seems to fall silent in midair. The coin magically evaporates. The box is empty.

Some matchboxes are made of thin wood. They won't buckle when you squeeze the ends. Use a paper matchbox. Any coin will work except a fifty-cent piece — it's too big. Nickels and quarters, because of their weight, slide out of the box like double-greased lightning.

The Big M

If you took the rattle, rattle out of this trick it wouldn't amount to much. That's because the sound misleads the audience into believing the coin is where it isn't. Magicians have a secret big word for this sort of thing — MISDIRECTION.

And when your hand goes to your pocket for the second rubber band (but really to get rid of the coin), that's misdirection too!

The Witch's Foot

"Have you ever seen a witch's foot?" Showing a twelve-inch ruler, you add, *"Well, that's a foot. And it's bewitched. Watch!"*

You lay the palm of one hand over the center of the witch's foot. It clings as if magnetized. But wait!

The ruler slowly lowers itself — and floats a couple of inches below your hand.

But wait again! As it floats, the ruler mysteriously trembles and shakes. *"Bewitched,"* you say. Then, *"That's enough, nervous spirit. Up, up!"*

The ruler rises back to your hand. And you take a bow.

Witches and nervous spirits have nothing to do with it, of course. You manage the entire routine with a cleverly concealed finger.

1. Begin by laying the ruler across someone's two hands. Then you grip your left wrist. *"I need a steady hand for this. Very steady."* Your left hand is palm up, so that everyone can see that it is empty.

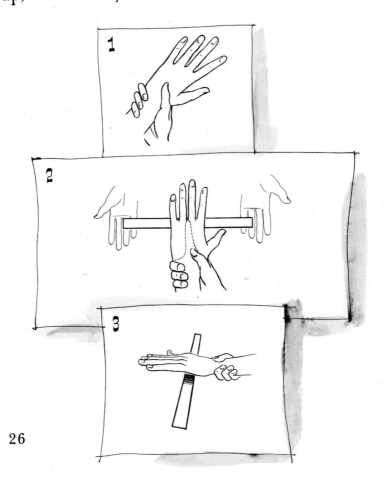

2. As you turn your left hand over (palm down), your right index finger slips off the wrist and against the palm. That's the trickery that makes this trick work. The secret movement is concealed by the left hand.

Look at the first drawing. See anything wrong? Have you ever noticed that most cartoon figures (even Mickey Mouse) are drawn with only three fingers and a thumb? The finger missing from your wrist passes unnoticed. Try it and see.

3. Rest your left palm over the center of the ruler. But your hidden index finger goes under the ruler. It presses the ruler against your left palm.

4. Now say, *"Please remove one of your hands."* The ruler should fall, but surprisingly it remains suspended.

5. *"And very gently remove your other hand."* Even more surprising! With no apparent support, the ruler clings to your palm.

6. And now it floats downward. How? Balanced on your hidden finger. It is easy to find the exact balance point — right under the six-inch mark.

Be aware that your friends must be looking *down* at this illusion. Lower your hands to make sure.

7. And here's the grand finale. Gently twitch your hidden index finger, balancing the ruler. It will shake and tremble — bewitchingly.

8. After commanding the witch's foot to rise, grip it in the left-hand fingers. As you turn the hand over (palm up), slide the concealed finger back around your wrist with the others. The trick is over — and you've nothing to hide.

You and the Great Swami

HERE'S A MIND-READING TRICK for you and your best friend to perform together. Your friend can wrap a towel around his or her head like a turban.

"May I introduce my friend, The Great Swami,"

you say, *"a reader of minds and a catcher of thoughts. Beware of what you think. The Great Swami tells all!"*

Send your friend into the next room while the audience selects four or five playing cards. They are returned to the deck, which is slipped back into its case and delivered to The Great Swami.

"Now each of you concentrate on your card. Send thought waves. Think hard! Think red or think black. Think of the number. The Great Swami must have absolute silence. When he has picked up your mental vibrations he will return. Are you ready, O Great Swami?"

"Ready, O Great Magician," says your friend, who reappears and tosses you the pack.

When you spread the deck several cards are upside down. And each is a selected card!

THE SECRET

Before you begin, turn the bottom card upside down.

Now have the audience select any number of cards. As you spread the pack between your hands don't expose the reversed bottom card.

"Look at your cards," you say. *"Don't forget what they are."*

At this moment, with everyone looking at the chosen cards, simply turn the pack over in your hands. Don't hurry the move. No one will notice.

The pack still appears to be back side up. Only you know that it is really face up with the back of a single card showing on top.

Keep the deck squared and one by one slip the selected cards into various portions of the pack. *"Don't let me see what they are,"* you say as you collect each card. Naturally they go face down into a face-up deck.

That means that they are already upside down! But it's too soon to spring that surprise.

And you must do something about that single, telltale top card. That's where The Great Swami comes in.

Slip the deck into its case and ask someone — anyone — to deliver it to the waiting mind reader.

While you deliver your spiel about The Great Swami, all he has to do is reverse the top card.

The trick is accomplished. He returns to the room, you spread the cards face up to show that several cards are reversed. Has the mind reading worked? Are they the chosen cards?

"*Raise your hand if The Great Swami has correctly received your thoughts.*"

With every card you now turn face up, a hand rises. And you and The Great Swami take a bow.

Trick Tip

It's best to use a pack of cards with a white border. You'll find it makes things easier to slip the chosen cards into the upside-down deck should the top (reversed) card slide a little out of position.

AaaaChooooo!

The Hanky-Panky Handkerchiefs

PERHAPS YOU'VE SEEN a magician pluck colorful silk
handkerchiefs from an empty tube. You can do it
too — without the special tube.

Pass out a newspaper. *"Choose any sheet,"* you
say. *"Examine it closely. I wouldn't trick you for the
world."*

Taking the single sheet of newspaper, show it on both sides. Then bunch it up in your hands and say a magic word.

After making a small tear in the newspaper ball you draw from it a string of "silks."

THE SECRET

The newspaper is completely untricked. The silks — as magicians call them — come from a most unexpected place. The pit of your arm!

You can find inexpensive, silklike handkerchiefs or scarves at the dime store. Tie them together, one end to another, and bunch them into a tight ball.

Tie the ball with a piece of fine black thread. Place the ball under the pit of your left arm. Draw the thread across your chest and attach the free end under your blazer. You can do this with a safety pin after measuring the length. Leave some slack in the thread.

Now you're all set to perform.

After you've shown the chosen sheet of newspaper on both sides, hold it outstretched in front of you. Release the arm pressure on the ball. It will swing free on the thread.

And if you bend the upper part of your body forward slightly the ball will dangle forward in midair. All of this, of course, is concealed by the newspaper.

It's a simple matter now to gather up the ball of silks as you make a loose ball of the newspaper.

Rip open the top, find the end of the silks and draw it up. Pause, letting the surprising bit of color show. Then continue pulling out silk after silk, just like the finest magician.

Magic Words

Casting wizards' spells is part of the fun of a magic trick. You may make up your own or try these incantations. They are guaranteed to be very powerful — unless the trick doesn't work right. In that case you can say that you cast the wrong spell.

Abracadabra!   *Alakazam!*

Hocus-pocus!   *Hokery-pokery!*

Shazam!   *Presto!*

Houdini in Your Pocket

THIS IS AN EASY, quicker-than-the-eye sort of trick.

"Have you ever heard of Houdini?" you ask. If not, explain that he was a great magician and escape artist. *"Houdini once walked through a brick wall. I know the secret. I can do it for you with two match sticks."*

You place one match between two fingers and say, *"Pretend that's a solid wall."* Behind it hold the other match. *"And pretend this one is Houdini."*

A moment later the Houdini match appears to pass through the wall match.

Hold one match between the left thumb and index finger. That's the wall.

The Houdini match is held a little differently. It is gripped firmly between the index and middle fingers of the right hand. The thumb, resting on top, can be lifted. That's how the trick works.

Link Houdini behind the wall.

Don't move the left hand. All of the action is in the right. As you draw it outward, lift the right thumb slightly as the two matches meet.

In this outward swing the wall match slips be-

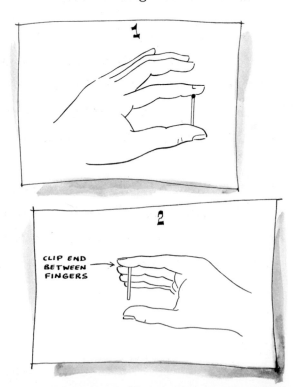

CLIP END
BETWEEN
FINGERS

tween the right thumb and the end of the Houdini match. The thumb returns to the match.

It's the work of an instant. The inside stick is now out. In fact, it happens so fast that your friends will miss it unless you focus their attention.

Say, *"Ready? Now don't blink an eye or you won't see how it's done. Houdini — do your stuff!"*

Pull your hands apart. Zip! Done!

The trick appears more magical if the matchsticks separate without a sound. Don't let them click.

Instead of wooden matchsticks you can do this trick with paper matches, toothpicks (of two different colors) — or even nails!

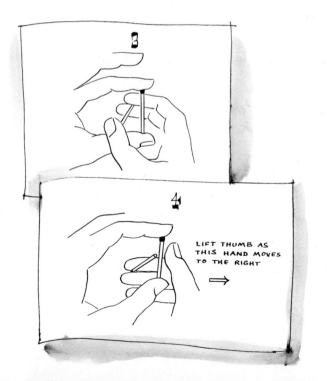

LIFT THUMB AS THIS HAND MOVES TO THE RIGHT

The Fool Me, Fool You Trick

"In this trick," you say, *"either you will fool me, I will fool you — or maybe we'll fool each other."*

Two decks of cards are used. Your friend selects a card from one pack. You choose a card from the other.

Your friend places his card under his shoe. You place your card under your shoe.

They turn out to be the same cards!

THE SECRET

Beforehand, arrange one deck with all the red cards on the bottom and the blacks on top. That will be YOUR deck, the one you handle. The other — your friend's deck — is untouched.

Spread your deck and have a card selected. If it is taken from the top half you know that it is black. *"Look at it and remember it,"* you say.

Then lift off more than half the pack, have the card returned and drop the balance of the deck on top of it. That places the black card in the red half of the deck.

Of course, if the card was chosen from the lower portion of the deck (red), be sure to replace it in the upper (black) portion.

Square up the deck and place it aside.

Offer your friend the other deck. *"Now you have me take a card."* Choose any card, look at it, and replace it. But don't bother to remember it. This is just for appearances.

Here's where the simple trickery comes in. *"Find the card in your deck that you selected from mine. Don't let me see it. Place it under your shoe. I'll find my card and do the same thing."*

But what you look for in your deck is your friend's card — the one in the wrong color section. Draw it out and put your foot on it. Your friend is picking from his own deck the card he picked in yours.

"So far we're even. Each of us is standing on the

card we chose. Now if you should change your card to mine, I'd be fooled. And if I could change mine to yours, you'd be fooled. Right? Do you know any magic words? Let's each say one."

Utter incantations.

"Now let's turn over our cards." Let your friend turn up the card first. Then flip over yours. Of course, they are the same.

Trick Tip

Sometimes a card will be selected from near the center of the deck and you won't be sure whether it is red or black. Here's what to do. Once you have divided the deck into reds and blacks, mark the top card of the lower packet. Do this on two opposite corners with a fine pencil point. You'll be able to spot it easily, no matter how faint it is, as you spread the cards and ask that one be selected.

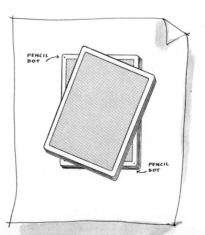

The Creepy, Crawly Thing

YOU WON'T BELIEVE how spooky-funny this looks until you try it.

Showing your left fist you say, *"I have a creepy, crawly thing in my hand."*

You pull a common rubber band through the top of your fist. *"That's my friend, Creepy, Crawly Cal-*

vin. I guess you know that creepy, crawly things live in the dark. They don't like light."

Creepy, Crawly Calvin seems to come to life. He begins to withdraw into your fist, twisting like a worm as he slowly sinks from sight.

Then comes the big fooler.

When you open your fist, the creepy, crawly thing has completely disappeared!

THE SECRET

Loop four or five rubber bands into a chain. Slip an end band over your left hand and up your arm, under the sleeve of your shirt or jacket. The rubber band must be tight around your arm, or fix it in place with a safety pin.

Now stretch the chain of rubber bands along the inside of your arm to your fist. The fist holds Creepy, Crawly Calvin, which is the rubber band at the free end of the chain.

You are ready.

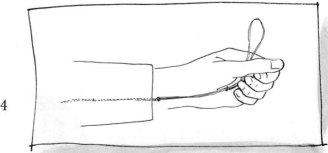

After explaining that you have a creepy, crawly thing in your fist, dig in and introduce Calvin.

The pressure of your fist holds Calvin in place. But when you ease up *very slowly*, the rubber band does the spooky-funny stuff. Finally, it slinks out of sight.

Gaze at your fist and say, *"Poor Calvin. Creepy, crawly things scare easily. If I say BOO! —"*

As you loosen your fist the stretched chain of rubber bands will whisk Calvin up your sleeve. The word BOO! covers the faint snapping sound.

Pause. Don't rush things. Still holding a fist, turn

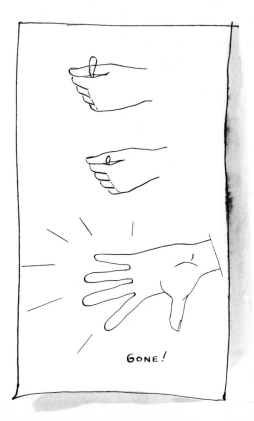

GONE!

it over. And one by one straighten your fingers to show your palm. The creepy, crawly thing is gone.

Grand Finale

Here's a different surprise ending for Creepy, Crawly Calvin. He doesn't disappear — he changes color!

Let's say that Calvin is a yellow rubber band. Before starting the trick, place a blue rubber band in your fist together with Calvin. Hold the loose blue band in the curl of your fingers so that it doesn't become entangled with the other.

Finally, when you let Calvin fly up your sleeve and open your fist, say, *"Look! He turned blue with fright."*

Watch the Penny!

HERE'S A QUICK, slick, sly trick with a double surprise at the end.

You show a penny in one hand and a nickel in the other. *"Watch! Watch! Watch the penny!"* you say.

Turning over both hands you slap the coins on a table. *"Did you watch? Did you keep your eyes on the penny? Which hand is it under?"*

Your friend guesses correctly. And no wonder. You haven't pulled the quick, slick, sly trick yet.

Pick up the coins and slap them down again. *"Which hand is the penny under?"* Let's say it appears to be the left.

You lift that hand — and surprise number one. The penny has vanished!

Surprise number two? Lift your right hand and there's the penny together with the nickel.

THE SECRET

You won't believe you can do this until you try it. The secret part happens so fast that it will fool your own eyes. Stop right now and get two coins.

Ready?

Show the penny on your left fingers and the nickel on your right. The backs of your hands should rest on the table.

Now turn your hands over, slapping down the coins on the table. Your hands should come to rest about two inches apart.

There's no magic to this, but practice slapping down the coins five or six times. That will educate your hands to the basic movement.

Now for the quick, slick, sly tricky part.

This time, as you turn your hands over — and at

the very last moment — give the penny a slight toss to the right. It travels only a couple of inches.

That's really all there is to it. For the right hand, in slapping down the nickel, will also slap down the penny, as shown in the drawing.

The tossed penny crosses the narrow gap between the two hands quicker than the eye can follow. Don't rush. Don't jerk. The penny will take care of itself in the slight throw you give it without breaking the rhythm of the hands.

Have you tried it? Amazing, isn't it! Even though this is a real sleight-of-hand trick, you can master it in less time than it takes to run around the block.

Dial-a-Trick

YOU CALL A FRIEND on the telephone and say, *"I'm going to read your mind* ~~over the~~ *telephone. You'll need a deck of cards. Any deck. I'll wait."*

Your friend returns to the phone and selects a card. Any card. A few moments later you name it.

Mind-boggling? Impossible? Read on!

50

Write the numbers from one to fourteen in a column on a piece of paper. Have it ready, with a pencil, when you dial your friend.

After he returns to the phone with a pack of cards, you give these instructions.

1. *"Before we begin, place a card to one side. Any card. But don't look at it. You might accidentally send me thought waves. We'll call it the Don't Look Card."*

2. *"Now shuffle and cut the deck. I've plenty of time. Let me know when you're finished."*

3. *"Ready? Choose a card from any part of the deck. Turn it face up on top of the pack and gaze at it. Concentrate hard. Be sure to remember what it is."*

4. *"Now cover it with the Don't Look Card — you didn't look, did you?"*

5. *"Okay. Now if the card you chose is an ace, draw one card from the bottom of the deck and place it on the Don't Look Card. If you chose a two, transfer two cards on top. A three, three cards, and so forth. Count a jack as eleven, queen twelve, king thirteen and the joker fourteen. I'll wait."*

6. *"Finished? The card you chose is now well buried. But I'm beginning to pick up your thought waves. Ah, I think I know your card. Except the suit. The color doesn't seem to be coming in. Are you concentrating on it?"*

The truth is you haven't the faintest idea what card was chosen — yet. Pick up your pencil. Your friend is about to tell you the card without realizing it.

7. *"Read the top cards off to me, one by one. I'll stop you when you reach your card. If I miss, just keep reading the cards. When you come to the Don't Look Card, call it out just like any of the others. But don't give me a clue with your voice, or pause or anything."*

As he begins calling out the top cards, *ignore* the first two. When he reaches the third card you jot it down at the top of your list of numbers. Use initials to save time — 5S representing the five of spades, QH the queen of hearts, and so forth.

When the number on your list matches the number of the card called, circle it. That's your friend's card!

But don't stop him. Let him read off four or five

extra cards. Then ask, *"You haven't passed your card yet, have you?"*

He will say that he has.

"Oh, of course. Now I can see it. I see a red card. a diamond. The six of diamonds." Or whatever the card really is.

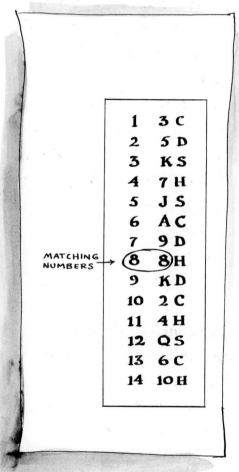

1	3	C
2	5	D
3	K	S
4	7	H
5	J	S
6	A	C
7	9	D
8	8	H
9	K	D
10	2	C
11	4	H
12	Q	S
13	6	C
14	10	H

MATCHING NUMBERS →

Are you wondering what the Don't Look Card is doing in this trick? Your friends will wonder about it too.

They'll think it is the clue to the secret. It diverts a part of their attention away from the *real* secret. You already know the word for this sort of thing. Misdirection.

Process of Elimination

At times a stray card will accidentally match up with the right number in your list. That's easily taken care of. You use what magicians call the Process of Elimination. Here's how:

If the matching cards on your list are of different colors, eliminate one by a guess. *"I get the impression of black spots. Is that correct?"* If wrong, you then know it is the red card.

If both cards are the same color, say, *"I get the impression of a high card."* If you guessed right, and the stray card is low, that eliminates it.

No matter what the combination of cards, you can eliminate by the differences between them. And oddly enough, it creates a stronger impression, in mind-reading tricks, to make an early mistake before finally succeeding.

The Toy Acrobat

You show a paper matchbook cover and say, *"Pretend this is a toy acrobat. Pretend it has a spring inside. I'll wind it up."*

You pretend to turn an invisible winding key. Make creaky sounds in your throat as though you were turning a real key.

Then set the acrobat on edge, on a table. When

you let go the match cover rolls over and does a somersault. It looks eerie.

Hand the toy acrobat to a friend to try. It falls flat. It won't somersault.

THE SECRET

Use an empty matchbook cover. Flatten the fold. Then shape the cover into a slight arc. Notice that the inside of the arc is on the flap side. That's important.

It's also important, when you set the cover on end, that the striking surface is at the top. It's the heavier end, and that's what makes the acrobat flip-flop, as you'll see.

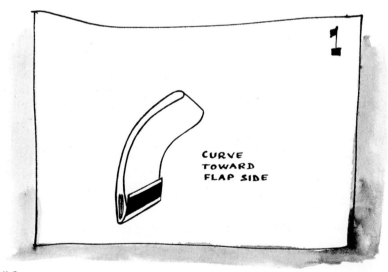

CURVE
TOWARD
FLAP SIDE

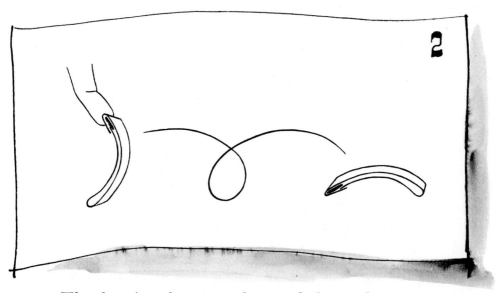

The drawing shows you how to balance the cover against a finger.

Ready? Now ease the top over *toward the outward side of the curve,* and let go. Don't try to flip or push it. The weight of the striking end will pick up momentum as it rolls and the packet will automatically somersault.

When others try it, they will almost always start with the scratching end at the bottom. It seems unnatural to balance the packet upside down, and rarely does anyone notice your starting position.

Even then, your friend is apt to allow the cover to fall in the wrong direction. With either mistake, the acrobat does a sad flop.

"The spring has run down," you say. "Rewind" and do it again.

Keep in mind that you must start with the heavy end up, put enough arc in the cover, and let it roll with the curve. After a few tries you'll discover how much shape to give it.

Those are your three secrets. As you offer the packet to someone to try, your fingers can bend out some of the curve. That will guarantee failure.

As you give it a rewind, put the curve back in. Success every time!

The Devil's Knucklebone

"Do you know what gamblers call dice? The Devil's Knucklebones. Here's a knucklebone that's full of the devil."

You show a die (that's the right word; dice, like mice, is plural). It's not tricked in any way. But brimstone and sulpher — every time you rub the die on your hand, the number of spots magically changes.

The first drawing shows you how to hold the knucklebone. Turn your hand over — palm up — to show the bottom. As you do so, your thumb rolls the die over to the next side. That changes the bottom.

Can't the monkey business be seen? Magicians have been doing this "turnover" fakery for a couple of hundred years and it hasn't been seen yet.

The reason is that the flipping over of the die is made invisible by the much larger movement of the hand.

Now for the devilish routine.

1. Show the six on top and the one on the bottom. No magic yet. Turn the hand palm down and rub the bottom spot on the back of your other hand. Say *"Beelzebub!"*

2. Now, as you lift the die and turn the palm up so that everyone can see the bottom, do the rollover. The one spot will have changed!

3. But you will want to show that the six is still on top, which it isn't. So you reverse the two movements. Swing your hand palm down. At the same time, roll the die back with your thumb. The six is back on top.

This is a puzzling trick, complete in itself. Once you get the roll down pat, you can add bafflement to puzzlement.

With the six always shown on top you make the

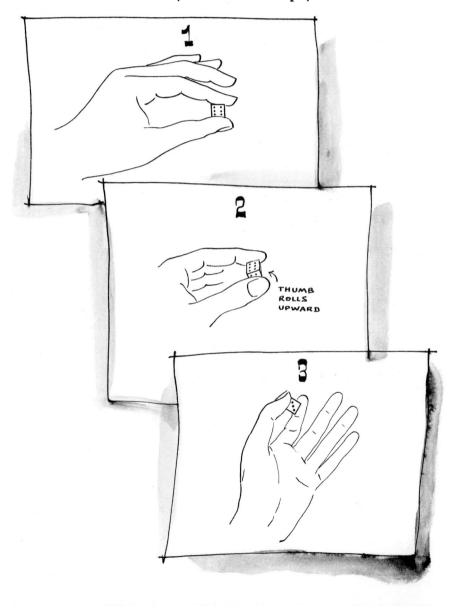

THUMB ROLLS UPWARD

bottom spots change again and again. You can cause anything to appear, from a two to a five.

These added bottom changes work themselves.

When you rub the die on the back of one hand, balance it there for a moment while you wave your other hand and say *"Beelzebub!"*

The trick is in the way you pick up the die. Grip it by two *other* sides. When you do the secret roll, a different number will appear on the bottom.

By continuing this rotation each time you pick up the die, you can run through all the spots except the six on top and the true bottom — the one spot.

Your Own Trick Deck
(And How to Make It)

THIS IS a fakey, funny-looking stunt, strictly for laughs. You spring a deck of cards through the air, from hand to hand, like the most skillful magician. *"This is the hardest trick I do."*

But everyone can tell that the cards are somehow strung together. And they'll holler and howl.

"The hard part is to fool anyone with it," you say, putting the deck aside and going on with a real trick.

THE SECRET

You need a stapler.

Using any old, dog-eared deck, staple the ends of the cards so that you make a sort of card accordian. Staple them two by two, alternating from top to bottom. Forty cards is enough, as the staples thicken up the deck.

Grip the completed pack between both hands. Then drop the lower hand, stretching the cards out, and slap them together again. Do it fast and noisily.

Show it to yourself in front of a mirror. Doesn't it look fakey-funny?

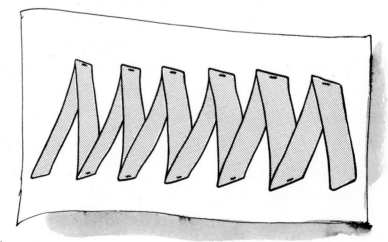

Rubber Band Bamboozle

You SLIP a red rubber band over two fingers. Then slip a yellow one over two other fingers. In less than the flick of an eye they change places.

Any colors will do, but let's say the rubber bands are yellow and red.

Place the yellow one over the first two fingers of your right hand. The red one goes over the other fingers.

Hold your hand palm down and snap the yellow band a couple of times. Say, *"Notice that this one is red."*

Your friend will protest that it is yellow. Say, *"No — this is the yellow one,"* and snap the red band.

Tip your hand so that the back is toward your friend. Snap the bands again from the palm side of your hand, and again call out the wrong colors.

While your friend is trying to set you straight, do this:

1. Draw back either band with two fingers of the left hand.

2. Pick up the other band with the same two fingers. Draw it back and spread the openings.

3. Close the right hand, curling your fingertips into the double opening.

The whole thing takes only a moment once you

get used to the moves. It is, of course, shielded by the back of your right hand.

Meanwhile, you say, *"Are you trying to tell me that the yellow rubber band is red, and the red one is yellow? One of us must be color blind. Here, point a finger at the one that looks yellow to you."*

As your friend's finger approaches your fist, open

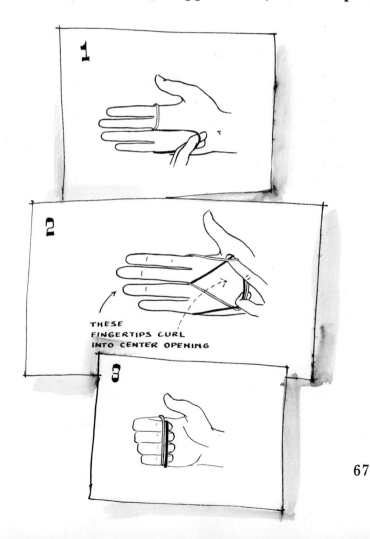

THESE
FINGERTIPS CURL
INTO CENTER OPENING

67

quickly and spread your fingers. The double illusion is startling. The yellow has instantly changed to red, for the two bands have reversed positions on your fingers.

"You may be right," you say, *"but that certainly looks red to me."*

Practice Made Easy

A pleasant time to practice finger tricks is while you are watching television. Especially during the commercials.

And look at yourself once in a while in front of a mirror. That will show you what the trick looks like to others. If you muff it there's no one watching — but you.

tock!

tick!

ding!

click!

thump!

The Lie Detector

IMAGINE THIS. You have a card chosen. Any card from anyone's deck. *"Now I'm going to take your pulse while I test some words on you. This will be a lie detector test. Changes in the beat of your pulse will tell all."*

At the end of the test you name the chosen card!

Of course, your friend's pulse has nothing to do with it. That's just fancy dressing for a very simple secret.

You learn the name of the card before you start the lie detector test. Here's how:

After the card has been chosen, hold it at arm's length with your thumb at the bottom and fingers along the top. The back is toward you.

"Look at your card again. Gaze at it hard. You mustn't forget it."

As you are saying this, and as if to call attention to the card, squeeze it a couple of times. That catches your friend's eye — movement always does.

But it also bends the card's face inward. And you are able to glimpse the bottom number and pip, as shown in the drawing.

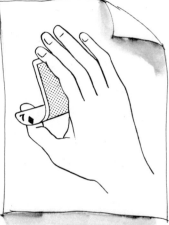

This will work only if you hold the card in your right hand.

Now place the card face down on the floor.

The rest is entertaining humbug — the fancy dressing.

With your thumb on the pulse of the one who selected the card, you start the lie detector test.

"Don't say a word. Just listen. Ready? Let's see how your pulse reacts to these colors. Red." Pause. *"Black."*

Adopt an expression of deep thought and uncertainty. Reveal nothing yet.

"Low card." Pause. *"High card."*

Then count slowly from ace through the king.

Name the suits: spades, diamonds, hearts, clubs.

Finally, *"Your pulse speeded up on red. At the number seven. The card you chose is the seven of diamonds."* Or whatever it is.

How can you miss?

The Alaska Fan

THIS IS right-before-your-eyes magic. You show two
short pieces of string. *"Abracadabra!"* In a flash they
join — becoming one long piece of string.

72

Hold up two pieces of string knotted together. *"You may think these are just two pieces of string. Nope. It's an Alaska fan. People in Alaska fan themselves with it. Unfortunately, this one is broken, but I think I can show you how it works."*

The two pieces of string are an illusion. You are really holding one long piece with a spooky knot in the middle. Here's how to make it:

Using soft string, cut a piece about two feet long. Near the center form a loop, draw a bit of string through it and tighten. You have made a common slip knot. That's easy.

Now cut an extra piece of string three inches long. Poke it through the loop. Snug the slip knot tightly against it by pulling on one of the strings.

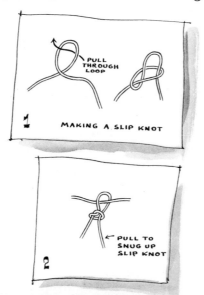

1   MAKING A SLIP KNOT

2   ← PULL TO SNUG UP SLIP KNOT

That's all. When you hold the long piece of string by one end, it will look like two pieces.

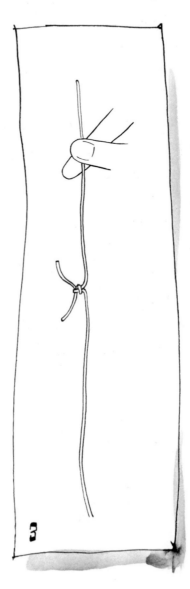

Now pick up the knot between the thumb and fingers, letting the string dangle.

Gaze at the lower ends and shake your head. *"One end is longer than the other. That's bad."*

Pick up a pair of scissors with your free hand and snip off the bottom end of one string, about half an inch. Then cut a piece off the top (the fake piece). Then return to the bottom, but never quite getting the ends even.

And, of course, the top ends are uneven too. Take another snip there. Go back and forth, snipping top and bottom.

The bottom trims are for misdirection. What you are *really* doing is destroying the fake piece at the top by snipping it away!

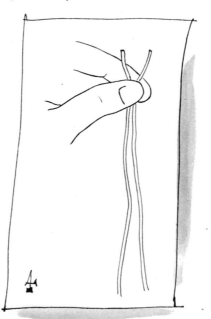

When you have cut it down to about an inch in length you'll find that you can tug it out of the slip knot between the blades of the scissors. Snip! The evidence falls to the floor.

The slip knot remains concealed between your thumb and fingers. Make a final trim at the bottom and put the scissors aside.

"That's better. Now I'll show you how to use an Alaska fan. You spin it like a jump rope."

Your free hand lifts one end of the string. The other fingers drop the knot and slide to the opposite end of the string. *Immediately* begin spinning the string.

In movement the slip knot is accepted as a knot with ends. Everyone can see it spin.

"In the frozen North people don't use fans to cool off. They want fans to warm up. You could spin an Alaska fan all day without kicking up a breeze. But you sure get warm doing this!"

You keep spinning.

"I can feel a breeze. It's that knot. Definitely a one-knot breeze. You'd freeze your nose with a broken fan like this. Don't try it. Unless you're a magician. Abracadabra!"

Pull the ends of the string taut and the slip knot will disappear.

Continue spinning a moment or two and then toss the string to your audience. The two pieces are now one!

Trick Tip

Try the Alaska fan trick with soft cotton clothesline, which you can find in the hardware store. The trick has a bigger look in case you want to perform for a large group.

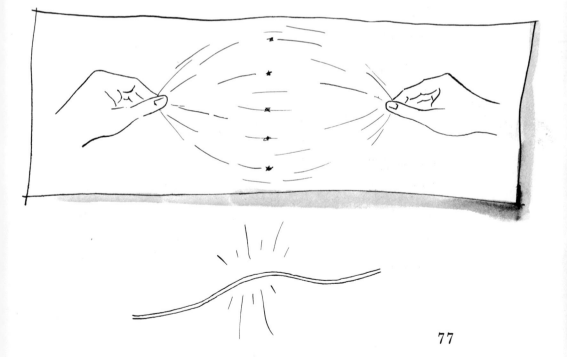

The Invisible Man's Money

PLUCKING COINS from people's noses was the first trick in this book. This last secret will enable you to follow it up with a bewildering baffler.

You flip the coin into the air a few times. *"This coin used to belong to the Invisible Man,"* you say. A moment later the coin, in midair, becomes invisible.

It reappears under your shoe. And it's the very same coin!

Sounds impossible, doesn't it? But all you have to learn is a sly and simple ruse.

1. You start with a catching game. After showing the Invisible Man's coin, toss it from the right to the left hand. Then flip it into the air and catch it with your right hand.

Repeat this tossing game two or three times. The coin travels in a sort of triangle. What you are doing is setting a pattern of movement for the eyes to follow.

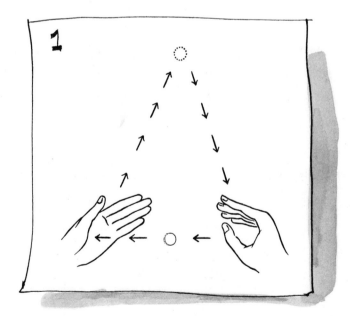

Say *"When the coin is up in the air it will vanish. But I've got to get it up high enough."*

2. Toss the coin a little higher. Your friends will think it *can't* be done, but they'll be watching the top of the triangle just in case.

3. Finally, as you catch the coin in the right hand, let it slip through your fingers and fall to the floor. This seems to have nothing to do with the trick. Even the finest magicians drop something now and then. But that's the sly and simple ruse.

4. For when you bend to pick up the coin, take a step or two so that the outside of your *right* shoe rests an inch or so beside the coin.

5. Now, as your *right* fingers reach the coin, the fingertips give it a small kick toward the shoe. Tip the foot slightly and the coin will disappear under the shoe.

Portville Free Library
Portville, N. Y.

6. Your friends, still unsuspecting, notice nothing wrong. For your right fingers pretend they have picked up the coin.

7. Straightening up, you go on with the catching game. But this time the right fingers merely pretend to drop the coin into the left hand. And the left fingers, curling, pretend they hold the coin. All of this pretending is easy, as you'll discover.

8. Look upward and give the left hand a hard toss. All eyes will follow the movement. It is uncanny, but the coin *seems* to vanish up in the air. Often people will swear they saw it leave your left hand.

9. Now pretend to pluck the invisible coin from the air. *"Got it. I don't want to lose it."* Reach into a pocket and withdraw the Invisible Man's invisible coin purse. Place the invisible coin inside. Place the purse in a right-hand pocket.

10. *"The trouble was that the Invisible Man's coin purse had a hole in it. Money was always slipping down into his sock. The sock had a hole and so did his shoe. See?"*

Shake your trouser leg and lift your shoe.

Ah, what wizardry! There's the coin.

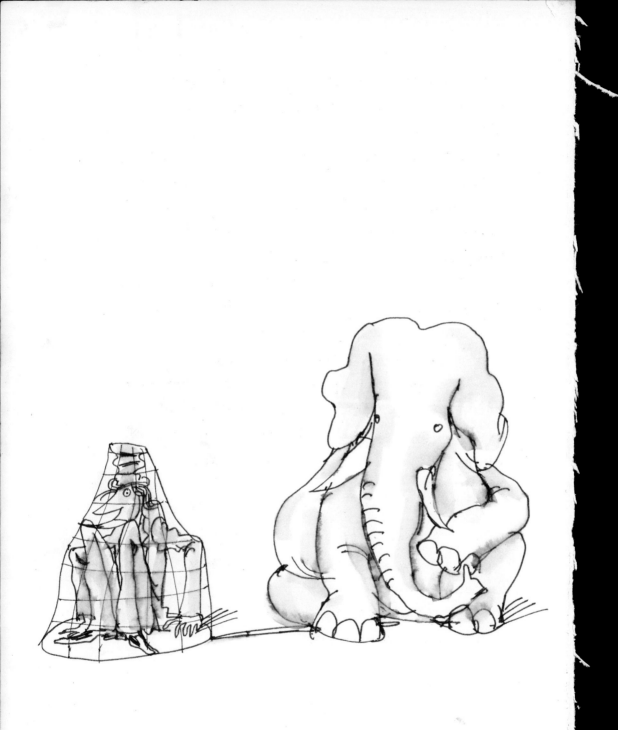

J
793.8
F

4 · 6

Fleischman
  Mr. Mysterious's
secrets of magic

Date Due

		7-18-14	

DISCARDED FROM THE
PORTVILLE FREE LIBRARY

PORTVILLE FREE LIBRARY

PORTVILLE, N. Y.

Member Of
Chautauqua-Cattaraugus Library System

BRO
DART   PRINTED IN U.S.A.